O JERUSALEM

A R Gurney

BROADWAY PLAY PUBLISHING INC
224 E 62nd St, NY, NY 10065
www.broadwayplaypub.com
info@broadwayplaypub.com

O JERUSALEM
© 2003 copyright by A R Gurney

All rights reserved. This work is fully protected under
the copyright laws of the United States of America.
No part of this publication may be photocopied,
reproduced, stored in a retrieval system, or transmitted,
in any form or by any means, electronic, mechanical,
recording, or otherwise, without the prior permission
of the publisher. Additional copies of this play are
available from the publisher.

Written permission is required for live performance
of any sort. This includes readings, cuttings, scenes,
and excerpts. For amateur and stock performances,
please contact Broadway Play Publishing Inc.
For all other rights contact Peter Franklin, William
Morris Agency, 1325 6th Ave, NYNY 10019,
212-903-1550.

First printing: May 2003
Second printing: April 2004
Trade edition printing: February 2005

I S B N: 0-88145-262-9

Book design: Marie Donovan
Word processing: Microsoft Word for Windows
Typographic controls: Xerox Ventura Publisher 2.0 P E
Typeface: Palatino
Copy editing: Sue Gilad

This play was first produced at the Flea Theatre in
New York City (Jim Simpson, Artistic Director;
Carol Ostrow, Producing Director), opening on
18 March 2003. The cast and creative contributors were:

SALLY . . . . Priscilla Shanks
HARTWELL CLARK . . . . .Stephen Rowe
AMIRA . . . . Rita Wolf
SWING ACTOR . . . . Chaz Mena
SWING ACTRESS . . . . Mercedes Herrero

Director . . . . Jim Simpson
Set & lighting . . . . .Kyle Chepulis
Costumes . . . . Sarah Beers
Sound . . . . Lindsay Jones
Props . . . . Beth Whitney
Onstage graphics . . . . David Prittie
Production stage manager . . . . Heather Prince

CHARACTERS & SETTING

SALLY, *an executive in the United States Information Agency*
HARTWELL CLARK, *Deputy Assistant Secretary of State for Near Eastern Affairs*
AMIRA, *a Palestinian activist*

SWING ACTOR, *to play other male roles; or they may be played by many actors*
SWING ACTRESS, *to play other female roles; or, again, many actresses may play these parts*
The speaking characters played are CYNTHIA, AMBASSADOR, ASSISTANT, F B I AGENT, OFFICIAL, CHRIS, ANNIE, & NATHAN.

Props, accessories, and costume pieces as needed, along with assorted furniture. Various large and legible cards or placards to be carried on and off, or placed on a portable easel which can be moved around the stage to indicate a particular location. All these elements should be handled by the actors. Somewhere upstage, an electronic device might indicate the date of each scene. In any case, the effect should be simple and economical, as if this were a touring production to be performed in a variety of venues.

for Jim Simpson with great appreciation

(At rise:)

(Time: The Future)

SALLY: *(Entering; to audience)* This is a play which was written soon after the terrible events of September Eleventh, Two Thousand and One. It was discovered some years later, among the personal effects of its author. Because it is a long, rambling and tormented piece...

(A thick, well worn-manuscript is displayed.)

SALLY: ...we make cuts and changes as we perform it, indicating these adjustments as we go along....

(A placard with the title is displayed.)

SALLY: The title—*O Jerusalem*—is obviously from the Bible, certainly from the Old Testament, and probably from the 122nd Psalm: "Our feet shall stand at thy gates, O Jerusalem." Some critics claim that the title is reverential. Others detect a sly note of exasperation. In other words, is *O Jerusalem* a prayer or a sigh? Every time we do this play, we wonder....

(HARTWELL CLARK *enters, wearing a gray summer suit, blue button-down shirt, and regimental tie, carrying a telephone.)*

HARTWELL: *(To audience)* The central character is a man named Hartwell Clark. He wears what many American businessmen wore during that period.

SALLY: *(Straightening his tie)* In fact, all our costumes strive for some degree of historical accuracy.

HARTWELL: (*To* SWING ACTOR, *who takes notes*) Please set up a conference call with Bill Price at Shell and Mark Milonzi at Texaco. Subject: moi. (*He looks at business documents, takes out his cell phone, talks importantly.*)

SALLY: You can see that Hartwell is an important executive of a large American oil company. He is now working out of the home office in Houston. During the play, he will get caught up in the turbulent politics of the Middle East, and in the attempt to do some good, he will ultimately lose his life....

(AMIRA *enters in a well-tailored suit.*)

AMIRA: (*To audience*) Another major character in our play is a Palestinian woman named Amira. Note that I am not wearing the "chador", the head-scarf which many Arab women wore at that time. This is because I comes from a distinguished Christian Palestinian family.

SALLY: Amira prides herself on her education and political activism.

AMIRA: (*On her cell phone*) Ana halwakti kharait iljareeda. Ana haimarra mahmoom ball. Ihna awzine sayartain isaaf lamustashfa Ramallah. Ma'a meen akhdar ahki min alsultta.

(*Two large cards are held up, displaying the translation. Card one: "I have just read the newspaper. I am disgusted once again." Card Two: "We will need at least two more ambulances for the hospital in Ramallah. Tell me whom do I call at the Authority."*)

SALLY: Amira also speaks excellent English, and is very much at home in the customs of the West. But her shoes give her away. They provide a slightly exotic touch, compared to the more practical footwear worn by American women. (*She indicates her own shoes.*) Such as my own. ...My character's name is Sally Mahoney. My mother is Jewish and my father Irish, so I grew up trying to negotiate between cultures. I now work for the United States Information Agency. My job is to convey American culture to other parts of the world.

(Sound: a few bars of Kate Smith singing God Bless America*)*

(Card: depicting Kate Smith, the American flag behind her)

SALLY: And to listen when other parts of the world answer back.

(Sound: a Muslim call to prayer)

(Card: an Arab mullah)

SALLY: And to negotiate there, when I have to.

(The cards are turned to face each other.)

SALLY: You'll notice that we use simple sound effects to create an atmosphere and occasional placards to designate a locale, and two other actors to play various other parts.

SWING ACTRESS: We hope that this emphasis on simplicity will remind you that theatre is an imaginative medium....

SWING ACTOR: ...which asks for your collaboration...

(As she hands off her card to him)

SWING ACTOR: ...as well as our own.

HARTWELL: *(On telephone)* So look, guys! Put in a good word for me with Bush, O K? Because, hey, remember: we're all in this thing together, right? *(Hangs up, goes off)*

(Time: January, 2001)

SALLY: The play begins early in 2001, soon after the inauguration of the second President Bush. The first scene originally took place in Hartwell's office in Houston, but we prefer to jump to when he comes home that night to his wife. *(She goes off.)*

(Card: an elegant Houston home)

(Music: New Age and relaxing)

(Swing Actress, *now as* Hartwell's *wife* Cynthia, *is being massaged on a table by* Swing Actor.)

(Hartwell *comes on.*)

Cynthia: *(Texas accent)* You're late. Per usual.

Hartwell: That's because I got an important call late in the day.

Cynthia: Uh-huh.

Hartwell: Guess who from.

Cynthia: Do I have to?

Hartwell: You might be surprised.

Cynthia: Suppose you do the surprising.

Hartwell: The President.

Cynthia: Of your company?

Hartwell: *(Saluting)* Of my country.

Cynthia: Georgie Bush?

Hartwell: The same.

Cynthia: He's inviting us to another barbeque?

Hartwell: He's inviting me to take a job.

Cynthia: What job?

Hartwell: Deputy Assistant Secretary of State for Near Eastern Affairs.

Cynthia: You might at least get the title right. It's "*Middle* Eastern", isn't it?

Hartwell: The State Department calls it "*Near* Eastern.*"

Cynthia: Why do they say that?

HARTWELL: *(Dismissing the masseur; taking over the massaging)* Maybe it's nearer than we think.

CYNTHIA: You're not serious.

HARTWELL: They've already started checking me out.

CYNTHIA: Is this because we know Dub-ya?

HARTWELL: I don't really know the guy, Cynthia.

CYNTHIA: You went to school with the man! Andover. Yale. Harvard Business School... The whole nine yards.

HARTWELL: Bush and I have a nodding acquaintance.

CYNTHIA: You must have done a lot of nodding to get this job.

HARTWELL: I asked for it, that's all.

CYNTHIA: *(Getting off the massage table)* You *asked* for it?

HARTWELL: And I got a few oil boys to run interference.

CYNTHIA: Pardon me, but you're not qualified, Hartwell.

HARTWELL: I know the area. I even speak a little Arabic.

CYNTHIA: You told them that?

HARTWELL: They already knew.

CYNTHIA: Oh right. Your little excursion after Yale. So what can you say in Arabic? How much is that rug? I'll have the cous-cous, please. Or just, "I love you"?

HARTWELL: Go easy, Cynthia.

CYNTHIA: Is she why you asked for the job?

HARTWELL: I haven't seen her in thirty years.

CYNTHIA: Then I wonder if you'd like to tell me why you suddenly decided to change careers.

HARTWELL: I've spent most of my life pumping stuff out of the earth, Cynthia. I figure it's time to put something back.

CYNTHIA: Oh please... *(To audience; no accent)* Here's where we've cut some clunky lines which remind us that at this time the Bush administration had turned its back on the Middle East. Which makes Hartwell's appointment at least possible, if not probable. *(To HARTWELL)* Have you told the kids?

HARTWELL: I left messages to call.

CYNTHIA: Maybe they will. Some day.

HARTWELL: This doesn't affect them much anyway.

CYNTHIA: It affects me, Hartwell. I thought we had settled down. I thought I was through following you around the globe...Lagos, Jakarta, Caracas, all for the love of Exxon...

HARTWELL: You'll like Washington.

CYNTHIA: I like Houston , Hartwell! Houston is home!

HARTWELL: Houston, we have a problem.

CYNTHIA: I like my kitchen, and my pool, and my book club. I like knowing the Bushes, and subscribing to the opera. I like going to the Astros, and....

HARTWELL: And making eyes at that guy in the next skybox...

CYNTHIA: Well I wouldn't say you've been squeaky clean over the years, puddin'.

HARTWELL: Here beginneth the standard spiel.

CYNTHIA: My therapist thinks it's time I developed a life of my own. Why do I always have to fall into line right behind you? Have you ever heard about roots, Hartwell? These are my roots. Right here. This time I have a right to—

HARTWELL: *(To audience)* This scene goes on forever, so let's cut to the American Embassy in Amman, Jordan.

CYNTHIA: Yes well you've never listened to me in your life!

(CYNTHIA exits angrily as HARTWELL looks after her.)

(Time: February, 2001)

(Sound: Arab music)

(Card: A fortress-like building with a large American flag in front.)

(SWING ACTOR comes on, now wearing a blue blazer. He is the American Ambassador.)

AMBASSADOR: Welcome to Jordan, Mr Secretary.

(He and HARTWELL shake hands.)

(For late arrivals:)

AMBASSADOR: Excuse me while I take care of some late arrivals. *(To arrivals)* Welcome, folks. This is Mr Hartwell Clark, who has just been appointed Deputy Assistant Secretary of State for Near Eastern Affairs. This is his first trip to Amman, Jordan, and we're giving him a small reception. *(After they are seated)* Again, welcome to Jordan, Mr Secretary.

HARTWELL: Mr Ambassador.

AMBASSADOR: *(Looking at him)* Say, by any chance did you play squash at Yale?

HARTWELL: Number three on the Varsity my senior year.

AMBASSADOR: Thought so. I played for Princeton. I took you on in New Haven.

HARTWELL: Who won?

AMBASSADOR: I did.

HARTWELL: Shit! *(Looking at him)* Hold it. Wait a minute. McAlister? ...McAlister...*Corky?*

AMBASSADOR: The same.

HARTWELL: Hiya, Corky.

(They shake again.)

AMBASSADOR: After the match, you invited me to a wild eggnog party at your fraternity.

HARTWELL: Was Bush there?

AMBASSADOR: Hanging out by the bar.

HARTWELL: Where else.

AMBASSADOR: People change.

HARTWELL: Let's hope.

AMBASSADOR: That was some party.

HARTWELL: I remember you and I were bird-dogging the same babe.

AMBASSADOR: Who won?

HARTWELL: I did.

(Sound: a cocktail party. Chattering voices, a piano background)

AMBASSADOR: We've arranged a small get-together in your honor. Want to say a few words?

HARTWELL: I'd rather listen. I'm hoping people have some suggestions.

AMBASSADOR: Suggestions? Here in the Middle East? Oh no. People have convictions.

HARTWELL: I'm all ears.

AMBASSADOR: *(Calling off)* Charlie! Take the Secretary around.

(HARTWELL *goes off as* AMIRA *comes on, stands watching him go.*)

AMBASSADOR: Yes? May I help you?

AMIRA: I wish to speak to Mr Hartwell Clark.

AMBASSADOR: Come with me. I'll introduce you.

AMIRA: *(Holding back)* Please, sir. No. I don't like crowds. Would you mind telling him that an old friend is here to see him.

AMBASSADOR: May I tell him your name?

AMIRA: Just say Amira. He'll know.

AMBASSADOR: Amira...I'll tell him. *(He goes off.)*

AMIRA: *(To audience)* And Hartwell comes on almost immediately.

HARTWELL: *(To* AMIRA*)* Amira? *(He attempts to embrace her.)*

AMIRA: *(Moving away)* Ah no. *(Holding out her hand)* This is the Middle East. Remember? Men and women shake hands. If that.

(They shake hands.)

HARTWELL: You're as lovely as ever, Amira.

AMIRA: And you are...what did you used to say? ...Full of bull.

HARTWELL: Hey watch it. I now represent the U S government.

AMIRA: Which sometimes is also full of the same.

HARTWELL: Easy now.

AMIRA: Yes, yes. I know. I am a guest. I had to pull many strings to be here.

HARTWELL: I'm glad you did.

AMIRA: I wasn't sure you'd remember.

HARTWELL: I remember everything. I remember Beirut. I remember auditing your course on Arabic poetry at the American University.

AMIRA: Ah, but do you remember any Arabic?

HARTWELL: I remember that the name Amira means "princess."

AMIRA: Good for you.

HARTWELL: I also remember asking you for a date.

AMIRA: You were very forward.

HARTWELL: You said yes.

AMIRA: Not immediately.

HARTWELL: Still, it was perfectly legit. You were an instructor. I was a Fulbright scholar. We were both technically on the faculty.

AMIRA: We were both very young.

HARTWELL: Is the university still there?

AMIRA: It's trying to be.

HARTWELL: What a great spot. I remember those red clay tennis courts overlooking the harbor.

AMIRA: And the King George Hotel down below.

HARTWELL: With that great room looking out over the sea.

AMIRA: And the American Sixth Fleet anchored off shore.

HARTWELL: That's what we called showing the flag.

AMIRA: Oh yes. We saw that flag.

HARTWELL: (*To* AMIRA) Do they still call Beirut the Paris of the East?

AMIRA: Not these days.

HARTWELL: "We'll always have Paris."

AMIRA: That's from one of your movies, isn't it?

HARTWELL: *Casablanca*, remember? We saw it together.

AMIRA: Ah yes.

HARTWELL: I felt like Bogart when we said goodbye.

AMIRA: Why?

HARTWELL: Because it was so tough to separate.

AMIRA: Was it really? For you? You had that girl to go back to.

HARTWELL: Which girl?

AMIRA: You always talked about a girl...what was her name? ...Sally, I believe.

HARTWELL: Sally? Oh hell. Sally's different.

AMIRA: You still see her?

HARTWELL: Now and then. But she's not why I left.

AMIRA: It's not important, why you left. The point is, you're here. Like that German officer in the movie arriving at the airport.

HARTWELL: *(Miming putting on gloves)* "Ve Chermans must become accustomed to all sorts of climates." I'm like *him*, not Bogart?

AMIRA: You're the occupying nation now.

HARTWELL: Oh hardly that.

AMIRA: Yes, well...

(Pause)

HARTWELL: *(Noticing her ring)* I see you're married.

AMIRA: Soon after you left.

HARTWELL: To a Palestinian gentleman?

AMIRA: You met him, actually. He was a friend of my father's.

HARTWELL: That older guy who was always hanging around your house?

AMIRA: That "older guy" happened to be a distinguished medical doctor.

HARTWELL: You married him?

AMIRA: My father asked me to.

HARTWELL: Is he here?

AMIRA: He's dead.

HARTWELL: I'm sorry.

AMIRA: Killed in Lebanon. When Sharon invaded.

HARTWELL: Oh boy... Any children?

AMIRA: Two. Just like you.

HARTWELL: How'd you know I had two children?

AMIRA: I read it in the *International Herald Tribune*.... Is one of your children a son?

HARTWELL: Yes.

AMIRA: Sons are important.

HARTWELL: Children are important.

AMIRA: Sons can do more.

HARTWELL: Mine doesn't do much.

AMIRA: Mine does too much.

HARTWELL: Meaning?

AMIRA: Oh it's a long story.

(Pause)

HARTWELL: So you live in Jordan now?

AMIRA: I live in Ramallah.

HARTWELL: What brings you here?

AMIRA: You, dear sir. You.

HARTWELL: Me?

AMIRA: Call it fate, then. Fate brings me here, as the Arabs say. Indeed, fate has taken me many places. Haifa first, where I was born. Lebanon, where I met you. Tunis, for a while. Then Lebanon again. Finally Ramallah. But now fate brings me to Jordan to meet an American secretary of state.

HARTWELL: Deputy. Assistant. Just for this area. Think low man on the totem pole.

AMIRA: I don't understand that expression.

HARTWELL: I'm a minor functionary, Amira.

AMIRA: You're an American official. That's enough.

HARTWELL: Enough for what?

AMIRA: Enough to do me a very great favor.

HARTWELL: Would you like to sit down?

AMIRA: Oh no. One never sits at these diplomatic affairs. People think you're negotiating.

HARTWELL: Nothing wrong with negotiations.

AMIRA: That depends on whom you negotiate *with*. Ask your friends in Israel. They'll tell you.

HARTWELL: Would you like something to drink? (*Begins to signal a waiter offstage*)

AMIRA: I don't drink. Remember?

HARTWELL: A coke, then? Something to eat? What would you like?

AMIRA: I'll tell you exactly what I'd like,
Hartwell Clark. I'd like to meet you in more
private circumstances.

HARTWELL: Good idea.

AMIRA: When do you leave Jordan?

HARTWELL: Tomorrow afternoon.

AMIRA: So soon?

HARTWELL: We have a complicated itinerary.
I am being introduced to my bailiwick. Damascus,
then Riyadh. Then Yemen. Then Cairo.

AMIRA: Not Tel Aviv?

HARTWELL: They come last.

AMIRA: Last but not least.

HARTWELL: The usual steps in the usual dance.

AMIRA: The usual dance of death.

HARTWELL: I hope it's not that.

AMIRA: It doesn't have to be... But tell me: will Tel Aviv
be where you stand on the steps of your great, noisy
silver plane and wave goodbye to us? Or do you plan
to make a short stop in Tunisia?

HARTWELL: How'd you hear that?

AMIRA: Oh, there's always talk in the Middle East.

HARTWELL: We're talking Tunisia, yes.

AMIRA: I have a married daughter there. And I've been
planning to visit her.

HARTWELL: When?

AMIRA: When you stop there.

HARTWELL: (*Laughing*) Oh Amira, you don't fool
around, do you?

AMIRA: Come to dinner at my daughter's. I'll send a formal invitation to your embassy there. Do you suppose they'll give it to you?

HARTWELL: I'll tell them I'm expecting it.

AMIRA: The gathering will be very small.

HARTWELL: That I like.

AMIRA: And very respectable.

HARTWELL: That I don't.

AMIRA: Don't tease, Hartwell. I'm serious.

HARTWELL: You always were.

AMIRA: You trust me, don't you?

HARTWELL: Yes I do, Amira.

AMIRA: Good. Because I trust you.

(AMBASSADOR *returns.*)

AMBASSADOR: I hate to interrupt but there's a businessman here who is desperate to meet the Secretary.

AMIRA: I understand.... Till Tunisia then. (*Shaking hands with both*) Thank you for a lovely party, Mr Ambassador.

AMBASSADOR: You can thank the American government for that.

AMIRA: I can thank the American government for many things.... (*She goes.*)

AMBASSADOR: (*Looking after her*) An old friend?

HARTWELL: More like a new one.

AMBASSADOR: Looks like you're back at the fraternity party, scoping out the babes.

HARTWELL: Don't I wish.

AMBASSADOR: She mentioned Tunisia.

HARTWELL: She wants me to meet her there on the way home.

AMBASSADOR: Don't, Hartwell.

HARTWELL: Don't?

AMBASSADOR: I just checked with Security. She's tied into some radical Palestinian organization.

HARTWELL: So?

AMBASSADOR: They're desperate these days. ...The failure of the Camp David peace talks... Sharon's visit to the Temple Mount... Now the new Intifada. Keep your distance, buddy.

HARTWELL: What is it they say in Washington? "I'll take that under advisement."

AMBASSADOR: *(Taking his arm)* The guy who wants to talk to you is over by the piano. He's interested in the gas deposits off the Gaza Strip.

HARTWELL: Oh really.

AMBASSADOR: Talk about gas. Something you know about.

HARTWELL: Right. I'll talk gas.

(They go.)

(Time: March, 2001)

(Card: the Washington Monument)

(SALLY comes on.)

SALLY: *(To audience)* We now go to my office at the U S Information Agency in Washington, D C.

(A couple of chairs are set up.)

SALLY: And I give a short speech about how Hartwell Clark and I go way back. We met on a blind date when he was at Yale and I was at Smith. Over the years, we have stayed—what?—good buddies. It's one of those corny, just-friends relationships between men and women that hang on forever, going nowhere fast. And frankly I find it slightly frustrating.

(SWING ACTOR *comes in, as her* ASSISTANT.)

ASSISTANT: The F B I is here about Hartwell Clark.

SALLY: Again?

ASSISTANT: They say it's important.

SALLY: Oh hell. Send them in.

(SWING ACTRESS *comes on as an* F B I AGENT, *carrying a notebook and wearing an officious jacket.*)

AGENT: Afternoon, ma'am.

SALLY: You're aware, I hope, that I was thoroughly interviewed when Mr. Clark was first nominated.

AGENT: Not thoroughly enough, ma'am.

SALLY: Explain, please.

AGENT: (*Checking notebook*) You told my colleague you had known Mr Clark since college.

SALLY: On and off. Yes.

AGENT: You didn't mention the Palestinian woman.

SALLY: No I didn't.

AGENT: You knew about her?

SALLY: I did.

AGENT: Why didn't you tell us?

SALLY: Slipped my mind.

AGENT: It slipped your mind?

SALLY: It was long ago and far away.

AGENT: It slipped your mind that a candidate for a major position in the Middle East once had a serious relationship with a Palestinian?

SALLY: Maybe I repressed it. How about that?

AGENT: Repressed it?

SALLY: Exactly. That means...

AGENT: I know what repression means.

SALLY: I'm sure you do.

AGENT: *(Referring to notebook)* Secretary Clark seems to be resuming the relationship with the Palestinian.

SALLY: Oh?

AGENT: He has made plans to meet her during a stopover in Tunisia.

SALLY: I didn't know that.

AGENT: *(Turning a page in her notebook)* Would you describe the Secretary as a "ladies' man"?

SALLY: Some people do.

AGENT: But you would not?

SALLY: He likes women. And women like him.

AGENT: Do you like him?

SALLY: Very much.

AGENT: Does he like you?

SALLY: We are good friends.

AGENT: Have you and he had a relationship?

SALLY: Depends what you mean by "relationship".

AGENT: I mean a sexual relationship.

SALLY: No.

AGENT: No?

SALLY: You have a problem with that?

AGENT: Yes, ma'am. I do. Considering the person involved.

SALLY: O K. How about this? Once upon a time there was a young nymph who rejected the advances of Apollo, the sun god. She refused to be simply another notch on his bow. So when he pursued her, she turned herself into a laurel bush—which is sort of thorny. Get it?

AGENT: No ma'am.

SALLY: The god took pity on her, and over the years, used her leaves to crown his successes. He liked to be crowned with her laurels. Get it now?

AGENT: No ma'am.

SALLY: Oh hell, neither do I. But I'll tell you this: after a while, she discovered it's not much fun being just a shrub.

(*Pause*)

AGENT: Let's move on.

SALLY: Yes let's.

AGENT: (*Checking notes*) Is Secretary Clark's marriage a happy one?

SALLY: I don't know.

AGENT: Has he ever made any disparaging remarks about his wife?

SALLY: He may be a ladies' man, but he's also a gentleman.

AGENT: Does he love his country?

SALLY: (*Dryly*) Don't we all?

AGENT: Do you?

SALLY: Do I love my country?

AGENT: That's my question.

SALLY: The answer is sometimes.

AGENT: You sometimes love your country. The country that has employed you for... *(Checks notebook)* ...twenty-three years. The country you represent at home and abroad? You love it only sometimes?

SALLY: That's what I said.

AGENT: *(Closing notebook, getting up)* Thank you very much, ma'am. *(Starts out, then stops, turns)* I happen to think that the United States of America is the greatest country in the world, and I love it every minute of the day and night.

SALLY: That's sort of why I don't.

AGENT: Have a good one. *(Exits angrily)*

SALLY: *(To audience)* Now here there was a flashback which took place in the seventies at a bar in New York called P J Clark's. In it, Hartwell sort of cries on Sally's shoulder because he misses Beirut. And she tells him she's involved with someone else, and secretly hopes this will upset him. But it doesn't seem to. He says that he's damn well going off to the B-school and the oil business, and has already met an oil heiress from Houston. So Sally decides to hold her nose and jump into marriage with a guy you sense is kind of a jerk.... The scene would only work with younger actors, so we decided to cut it. *(Then briskly)* So. On to Tunisia...

(A map of the Roman Empire at the peak of its power is brought out.)

SALLY: Which...is...right about...here... *(Pointing)* See? ...This was Tunisia during the Roman Empire.... They say it's very lovely, and sitting somewhat on the

sidelines from the Middle Eastern Dance of Death....
(*She goes off.*)

(*Time: April, 2001*)

(*Sound: Arabic music; sounds of waves*)

(*Moonlight: the sense of a balustrade*)

(*Card: the sea, the sky, a crescent moon*)

(HARTWELL *and* AMIRA *come on.* AMIRA *wears something more exotic.*)

HARTWELL: Great dinner.

AMIRA: You still like lamb, I notice.

HARTWELL: I still like yours.

AMIRA: My daughter cooked it.

HARTWELL: She had a good teacher.

AMIRA: (*Indicating the view*) Behold the Mediterranean Sea.

HARTWELL: Beautiful, as always.

AMIRA: The Romans called it "*mare nostrum.*" Our sea. I'm amazed you Americans don't call it yours.

HARTWELL: You'll notice we don't.

AMIRA: That's true. You are much more possessive about the Pacific.

HARTWELL: (*Putting an arm around her*) Lighten up, Amira.

AMIRA: (*Breaking away*) Did you know that Tunisia is the seat of ancient Carthage.

HARTWELL: I'd forgotten that.

AMIRA: (*Pointing*) The old city was off there, to the right, before the Romans destroyed it. *Carthago delenda est.* Carthage must be destroyed.

HARTWELL: The Romans said that?

AMIRA: They not only said it, they did it. Then they sowed the fields with salt so nothing would grow.

HARTWELL: Why?

AMIRA: Because Carthage surprised them with a sneak attack. Suddenly, there was Hannibal! Right before the walls of Rome! He had come around over the Alps on elephants. It frightened them terribly. So they hit back, hard.

HARTWELL: And won, didn't they?

AMIRA: Totally. They wanted everything, so they conquered everything. And sat on it all, for over six hundred years.

HARTWELL: Do you think America wants to conquer Tunisia?

AMIRA: Worse. You want to "develop" it. Tunisia is one of the few places left on the Mediterranean that remains relatively untouched. So you'll probably globalize it. And sew its fields with insecticide.

HARTWELL: *(Looking around)* Where are the others? Aren't they joining us?

AMIRA: I told them we needed to be alone.
(At prop table) Coffee?

HARTWELL: Decaf?

AMIRA: Of course not.

HARTWELL: Thank God.

(AMIRA *pours coffee into demitasse cups.*)

HARTWELL: Know something, Amira? My wife thought I asked for this job in order to see you.

AMIRA: Oh?

HARTWELL: I said, hell no. I wanted to do some public service. But then I began thinking what if I bumped into you again? And what would happen if we did? So maybe, deep down, that's why I applied for the job after all. Not for some fancy dream about doing good. Maybe just to see you. Because we had a good thing going, didn't we, Amira? Back then? Much better than what I've got going back home. Going fast, I might add. What do you think?

AMIRA: I think that when you get to our age, the past always looks better than the present. *(Bringing him coffee)* Would you like a cigarette? It's not a capital crime as it is in the States.

HARTWELL: I don't smoke.

AMIRA: You used to. Always.

HARTWELL: After dinner.

AMIRA: After lots of things.

(HARTWELL *suddenly kisses her. She breaks away.)*

AMIRA: That's not why I asked them to leave us alone.

HARTWELL: Damn. Strike two.

AMIRA: Seriously, Hartwell, I have to tell you something about your country.

HARTWELL: Everyone has been telling me something about my country.

AMIRA: I doubt if you've heard this.

HARTWELL: Try me.

AMIRA: Your country's in great danger.

HARTWELL: That I've heard, Amira. The bombings in Riyadh and Kenya. The destroyer *Cole*... That's all we talk about, everywhere we go.

AMIRA: This is very different.

HARTWELL: How is it different?

AMIRA: *(Looking out and down)* Who is that man down there?

HARTWELL: My security, I'm afraid. His name is Spencer. *(Waves)* Hiya, Spence!

VOICE: *(From off)* Yo!

AMIRA: Is he carrying one of those listening devices?

HARTWELL: Amira, I promise. No.

(Pause)

AMIRA: There is going to be a major terrorist attack on your country. Worse than anything that's happened so far.

HARTWELL: How will it be worse?

AMIRA: Because it will take place on your home soil. Many Americans will be killed.

HARTWELL: How did you learn this stuff?

AMIRA: From my son. Who travels a great deal in the Middle East.

HARTWELL: Doing what?

AMIRA: Business. Of various kinds. And he keeps hearing these same rumors. Again and again.
Of this major attack, coming your way.

HARTWELL: There are always rumors. You should see my daily briefings.

AMIRA: These are more serious.

HARTWELL: Why?

AMIRA: Because my son works for a serious organization.

HARTWELL: Named what?

AMIRA: Hamas.

HARTWELL: Hamas is your son's business?

AMIRA: Yes. Since recently. Yes.

HARTWELL: And Hamas now wants to attack
Americans?

AMIRA: Hamas wants to end the Israeli occupation of
Palestinian lands. But they hear of others who want to
blow up America. Unless you do something about it,
Hartwell.

HARTWELL: I'll tell you exactly what I can do. I can put
your son immediately in touch with our intelligence
people. They will send his information on to
Washington, to be coordinated with what is known
already. Then, if the threat looks even remotely
credible, we'll take steps to prevent it.

AMIRA: My son won't talk to American intelligence
people.

HARTWELL: No?

AMIRA: He feels that would be giving aid and comfort
to the enemy.

HARTWELL: But he's willing to talk to me?

AMIRA: He might, if....

HARTWELL: If what?

AMIRA: If the enemy behaved more like a friend.

HARTWELL: Goddammit, Amira, as you may have
noticed, I had the vague hope that you and I were
meeting tonight to turn back the clock. I looked
forward to a good meal, which I had, and some
pleasant reminiscences, which again we've had,
and I even had fantasies that we might pop into bed,
just to see if we could sound a few of the old chords.

AMIRA: I had those thoughts as well.

HARTWELL: I'm wondering if you did, Amira, because this evening has rapidly become what *my* son would call a total turn-off. It now appears to be dedicated to the proposition that I do some favor for your son, the terrorist.

AMIRA: He has a proposal for peace in the Holy Land.

HARTWELL: We don't call it the Holy Land these days....

AMIRA: Perhaps you should! Because it happens to be holy to others beside the Jews.

HARTWELL: Whatever it's called, there are plenty of peace plans already on the table.

AMIRA: This plan might be different.

HARTWELL: Oh I see. Devised by your son the terrorist.

AMIRA: Don't keep calling him that! My god! You Americans throw that word around the way you did with the word "communist."

HARTWELL: Oh. Sorry. Your son the freedom-fighter.

AMIRA: It's a good plan, actually. I helped him with it. In hopes he might leave Hamas.

HARTWELL: I'm sure there are a number of distinguished Palestinians you could take it to.

AMIRA: It will never get anywhere unless you propose it, Hartwell.

HARTWELL: Why me, of all people?

AMIRA: Because you're an American Secretary of State.

HARTWELL: Deputy Assistant, please.

AMIRA: And a friend of Bush. You went to school together.

HARTWELL: I'm beginning to think we learned different things.

AMIRA: Oh Hartwell. Please.

HARTWELL: Dear lady, I can't suddenly scamper back to Washington with a peace plan tucked under my arm. I may be a baby in this business, but I know things don't work that way.

AMIRA: But couldn't you propose it as a—what is that expression?—"a trial balloon", at least to your staff?

HARTWELL: Possibly.

AMIRA: And if they liked it, couldn't you take it on up to Powell and Bush?

HARTWELL: Maybe.

AMIRA: If my son could be sure that you'll take these tiny little steps, then he'll be here in half an hour to tell you all he knows about the planned attack on your native land.

HARTWELL: Your son's here? In Tunis?

AMIRA: I asked him. He's waiting to see you.

HARTWELL: I'd better go. *(Calls out and down)* Spence!

VOICE: Yep?

HARTWELL: Bring the car around. Sound the horn and I'll come right down.

VOICE: *(From off)* Yes sir!

AMIRA: You said you trusted me.

HARTWELL: I don't trust your son.

AMIRA: He could be yours, you know.

HARTWELL: Oh come on.

AMIRA: I could have been pregnant when you left.

HARTWELL: But you weren't.

AMIRA: He was born eight months after I was married.

HARTWELL: Oh hell, Amira! Let's compare dates.
I left Beirut that August, and you got married when?
Come on. Dates, please. When was he born?

AMIRA: Very well. He's not your son.

HARTWELL: Thank you.

AMIRA: But sometimes I like to think he is.

HARTWELL: Why?

AMIRA: Because I loved you.

(Sound of a car horn)

HARTWELL: There's my ride. *(Shaking hands with her)*
It's been an interesting evening, Amira. I'll say that.
(He starts out.)

AMIRA: He's your son in spirit at least....

HARTWELL: Oh now it's in spirit....

AMIRA: In spirit. Yes. For the past fifty years, you
Americans have produced offspring all over the
world—passionate young men and women inspired by
your ideas of freedom and justice, and desperate to put
them into practice. You should be helping them along.

HARTWELL: You may have a point.

AMIRA: Do you remember the ending of *Casablanca*?

HARTWELL: Bogart says goodbye.

AMIRA: But doesn't he then start a beautiful friendship
with the Free French?

HARTWELL: Right. Sort of. Yes.

AMIRA: You could do that with my son.

HARTWELL: *(kissing her)* Strike three and I'm outa here. *(He goes.)*

AMIRA: *(Calling after him)* If you change your mind, Hartwell, I'm sure your ubiquitous C I A can tell you exactly where to reach me. *(She goes.)*

(Time: May, 2001)

(Sound: Soupy hotel-lobby music)

(SALLY comes on.)

SALLY: *(To audience)* Here's where I at last get to play a scene with lover boy. Let me remind you that my job with the U S I A is to tear around the globe, inspecting American libraries, arranging lectures and exhibitions, and extolling the virtues of American democracy. *(Takes a briefcase from the prop table)* This summer I happened to be in Dubai, on the Persian Gulf.

(Placard: an ad for Dubai indicating: a forest of oil wells)

SALLY: I had a couple of duties to perform here. First, I had to deal with the fact that a boxed set of *Sex and the City* videos, destined for Thailand, had somehow found its way onto the shelves of our local library.

(SWING ACTOR, wearing Arab covering, disapprovingly displays the cover.)

SALLY: See? Slightly more sex than city. The local mullahs were up in arms. I removed the offending material....

(She dismisses the SWING ACTOR.)

SALLY: ... made an official apology, and then stopped by the Dubai Hilton to accomplish task number two. A conference of an OPEC Planning Committee was in full swing ...

(Placard of Dubai is reversed, revealing an announcement of an OPEC conference on the reverse side: "Guest Speaker: Mr. Hartwell Clark")

SALLY: ...and Hartwell was finishing up his keynote address.

(Sound: applause and then the general murmur of male voices)

(Two chairs)

SALLY: There was a coffee break.

(She is handed her coffee in a Starbucks-type cup, as HARTWELL *comes on, notices her.)*

HARTWELL: I thought I noticed you, hiding in back. *(He kisses her.)*

SALLY: Hiding? I stand out like a sore thumb— being the only woman around.

HARTWELL: *(Indicating off)* Oh yes? What about Madame Surabaya from Indonesia? Or that Nigerian lady with the gorgeous beach towel on her head?

SALLY: *(Looking)* You're right. They're more noticeable than I am.

HARTWELL: Except they're not.

SALLY: I hope that's a compliment.

HARTWELL: You're still a knockout, Sal.... I'll get coffee. *(He goes off.)*

SALLY: Here there was another flashback about when we last met. I was working at our embassy in Indonesia, and Hartwell was there working for Exxon, and he asked me to sneak off to Bali for a naughty weekend— until I reminded him we were both married.
(To HARTWELL*)* "We have these spouses," I said.

HARTWELL: *(Returning with coffee)* Yes.

SALLY: So that was that. It's a sweet scene, actually,
but the other actors felt it slowed things down,
so we had to cut it.

(They sit.)

SALLY: How's Cynthia?

HARTWELL: Fine, I guess....

SALLY: You guess?

HARTWELL: How about Mark?

SALLY: We split up.

HARTWELL: Again?

SALLY: He said he was tired of being married to a
wandering Jew.

HARTWELL: I keep forgetting you're Jewish.

SALLY: My mother is.

HARTWELL: That's what counts, isn't it? The mother
being.

SALLY: It's supposed to.

(He pulls up a couple of chairs. They sit and drink coffee.)

HARTWELL: Did you hear my speech?

SALLY: The tail end of it.

HARTWELL: What did you think?

SALLY: Money says you wrote that speech all by
yourself.

HARTWELL: How could you tell?

SALLY: You talked about conservation.

HARTWELL: I did, didn't I?

SALLY: Conservation? Under Bush and Cheney?
To a bunch of oil ministers?

HARTWELL: I threw it in at the last minute.

SALLY: You even said you hated S U Vs.

HARTWELL: I do. Except my own.

SALLY: Same old Hartwell. Mixed signals, up and down the line.

HARTWELL: Mixed signals? Never to you.

SALLY: Especially to me.

HARTWELL: I'll probably catch hell back in Washington. Or worse: they won't know or care.

SALLY: Oh they'll know. And care, too, I promise you. That's why I stopped by. I bring a message from Howard.

HARTWELL: Howard Stone?

SALLY: He knew I'd be coming here. And he reminded me he's been your office manager for over twenty years.

HARTWELL: He's a dear man.

SALLY: He's a worried man.

HARTWELL: About what?

SALLY: You.

HARTWELL: Me?

SALLY: He says you are the subject of comment in the corridors of the State Department.

HARTWELL: For example?

SALLY: For example... *(She rummages in her purse.)* I made some notes here. If I can find them. See how bureaucratic I've become? *(Finds a piece of paper)* These are what we call "talking points." Mind if I talk from them?

HARTWELL: Go ahead.

SALLY: There is a certain concern about your Palestinian friend.

HARTWELL: Oh well yes. I figured that.

SALLY: They think you're having an affair with her.

HARTWELL: I'm not.

SALLY: Promise? No, strike that. It's none of my business.

HARTWELL: I promise, Sal.

SALLY: *(Returning to her notes)* People are aware that when you were last in New York you had lunch with a member of the Palestinian Observer delegation to the U N.

HARTWELL: I later had lunch with someone from the Israeli consulate.

SALLY: They are concerned about these lunches.

HARTWELL: They think I'm eating too much?

SALLY: They think you're stirring the pot too much.

HARTWELL: Shit, Sal! I'm just trying to learn something....

SALLY: O K, O K, O K. *(Checking her notes)* Howard also came across a confidential memo from someone in the Defense Department, saying things about you.

HARTWELL: What things?

SALLY: Saying—apparently that you were.... *(Reads)* "...no friend of the Jewish people."

HARTWELL: Oh for Chrissake!

SALLY: It pointed out your fraternity at Yale didn't admit Jews.

HARTWELL: Neither did Bush's.

SALLY: It also said your tennis club on Nantucket
is restricted.

HARTWELL: Not anymore. Thanks partly to me,
I might add.

SALLY: And it said that your father was replaced by
a Jewish gentleman at Morgan Stanley, which made
you resent Jews ever since.

HARTWELL: WHAT? That's a goddam lie, Sally!

SALLY: It sums things up by saying.... Howard wrote a
lot of this down.... (*Reading*) You are a typical example
of the old school WASP who has been "marginalized"—
that's the word, apparently—"marginalized", as the
Jews have risen in power. Which is why you identify
with the Palestinians.

HARTWELL: Who wrote that fucking memo?

SALLY: I won't tell.

HARTWELL: Is he Jewish?

SALLY: No she isn't.

HARTWELL: She?

SALLY: That's just to throw you off.

HARTWELL: My father retired from Morgan Stanley!
It was totally his own choice!

SALLY: O K.

HARTWELL: And I have a great many friends who
are—my Best Man in my wedding was—... (*Stops*)
I won't go there.

SALLY: I wouldn't.

HARTWELL: Christ, this pisses me off. (*Gets up,
paces around*)

SALLY: Sit down. Everyone's looking at you.

HARTWELL: I don't want to sit down.

SALLY: I told them back at the State Department that you took *me* out at college, and I'm as Jewish as they come.

HARTWELL: Hardly that.

SALLY: All right, all right.

HARTWELL: But I appreciate this, Sal. What do you think I should do?

SALLY: Speaking as a Jew, I'd say spend a little more time in Tel Aviv.

HARTWELL: O K. Fair enough. And?

SALLY: And speaking from long experience in government, I'd say back off from the peace process thing.

HARTWELL: Why?

SALLY: Because you could get killed, Hartwell.

HARTWELL: Killed?

SALLY: In the sense that you could lose your job. And Howard could lose his. And neither one of you can go back to Exxon-Mobil, or whatever they call themselves these days. You've burned those bridges, buddy pal, especially when they hear that you're now for conservation. You'll be out in the cold, dear heart.

HARTWELL: Maybe so. *(Pause)* But I'm going to reject your advice, Sal.

SALLY: Knew it.

HARTWELL: Everything you've told me just makes me realize I'm going in the right direction! Because it's that kind of prejudice, Sally, that kind of stereotyped thinking by the numbers which is causing so much of the trouble out here and back home. I mean, Christ!

When in God's name are they going to realize that we
are all in this thing together?

SALLY: May I quote you on that?

HARTWELL: Yeah well when you get back, tell Howard
thanks, and I'm sorry, but this just makes me want to
dig a little deeper.

SALLY: Spoken like a true oil man.

(Sound: a loud buzzer. Then the murmur of men's voices)

HARTWELL: The conference is cranking up again.

SALLY: You'd better get back. You're the guest of honor.

HARTWELL: How about dinner tonight?

SALLY: Can't.

HARTWELL: Sure you can.

SALLY: I can not, Hartwell. I'm due to visit our library
in Cairo. Someone there has defaced the complete
works of Philip Roth.

HARTWELL: Fly down tomorrow. Stay here tonight.
Things are pretty much over with Cynthia and me.

SALLY: I thought you were fanning your old flame.

HARTWELL: Strictly business.

SALLY: Yeah, yeah. Tell me another.

HARTWELL: Really, Sal. I'm serious. I'm feeling a little
lonely out here.

SALLY: Sorry, Hartwell. I still refuse to be just another
conquest on your march to glory.

(Another buzzer)

*(*SALLY *gives him a quick kiss.)*

SALLY: Now get going. The oil cartels of the world
await your word.

HARTWELL: *(To audience)* At this point in the play, Sally turns to the audience and gives her famous speech.

SALLY: *(To audience)* She says there is more creative energy, and open argument, and freedom of spirit in one square mile of the land of Israel than in all the Arab countries combined.

HARTWELL: The speech has been quoted so often in magazines and newspapers that we thought it was redundant to repeat it here. *(He goes off.)*

SALLY: *(Looking after him)* Besides, frankly, it's a hard speech to do. Because whenever she does it, you have the feeling that she really isn't thinking about Israel at all. ... *(Then brightly)* Aaanyway, we also cut most of the next scene, where Hartwell Clark is called on the carpet in Washington, though it ends with an exchange that is worth presenting.

(Time: June, 2001)

(Placard: Washington monument)

*(*SWING ACTOR *comes on as a State Department* OFFICIAL. *He and* HARTWELL *sit at a table.)*

OFFICIAL: *(Southern accent; handing him back a document)* Frankly, Hartwell, I'd cut back on your boondoggles to the Middle East.

HARTWELL: Boondoggles?

OFFICIAL: "Official visits", then. Stay home for a while. Get to know the territory. I've got season tickets to the Redskins. I'll bring Rosalie and you bring your Missus....

HARTWELL: The "Missus" prefers the Astros these days, Billy.

OFFICIAL: You're doing too much travelling, buddy.

HARTWELL: Who's counting?

OFFICIAL: The taxpayers are.

HARTWELL: As I told that reporter from *Time*, "I'm leaving no stone unturned in my quest for peace."

OFFICIAL: In your quest for a piece of ass, looks like.

HARTWELL: I don't give a shit how it looks, Billy. I may be making headway out there. *(Handing him the document to sign)*

OFFICIAL: Hartwell, old friend. How many times have we heard that, over the years? Kissinger, Clinton, Jimmy Carter... *(Handing back document)* We think it's best just to leave it alone.

HARTWELL: *(Getting up; taking document)* I wish the Jews had picked somewhere else for their promised land.

OFFICIAL: Hold on there, pal. I'm born-again now, thanks to my Rosalie. I happen to believe that God picked it for them.

HARTWELL: Tell me, Billy: why do you think He did that?

OFFICIAL: So the Jews could prepare the way for the Second Coming of Our Lord Jesus Christ.

HARTWELL: Do you suppose the Jews are aware of that?

OFFICIAL: They will be, when they convert to Christianity.

HARTWELL: The Arabs think God has a different agenda, Billy.

 OFFICIAL: I don't know what the Arabs think, Hartwell.

HARTWELL: Let me tell you what I think, Billy. I think God may have sold the same piece of property to a number of different clients. He could use a refresher course in real estate.

OFFICIAL: That, my friend, is blasphemy! "Thou shalt burn in hell and be set upon by Devils!" *(Turns to the audience)* And then his wife asks him for a divorce.

(He goes as CYNTHIA *comes on with divorce papers.)*

CYNTHIA: Goddamn you, Hartwell! *(Turns to audience; no accent)* I'm just doing the end of the divorce scene.... *(To* HARTWELL*)* Goddamn you, Hartwell! How come you're walking off without a fight?

*(*HARTWELL *walks off; she calls after him.)*

CYNTHIA: Here you are, letting me have the whole store while you dicker over every square inch for those fucking Palestinians! *(To audience)* That's it. *(She goes off.)*

(Time: August, 2001)

(Sound: exotic Middle Eastern music)

(Card: The Dome of the Rock in Jerusalem under a starry sky)

(A rug and some pillows)

*(*HARTWELL *comes on, still carrying the Peace Plan document. He removes his shoes.)*

*(*AMIRA *comes on.)*

AMIRA: Well?

HARTWELL: *(Looking around)* Nice digs.

AMIRA: This house belongs to a family that has lived here for generations. They were recently notified by the Israeli authorities to sell within six months.

HARTWELL: I'm sorry.

AMIRA: Yes, yes. I keep telling you these things, and you keep telling me you're sorry.

HARTWELL: I'm also sorry for something else, Amira.

AMIRA: Oh?

HARTWELL: The answer is no.

AMIRA: No to what?

HARTWELL: No to everything.

AMIRA: From whom? Powell? Cheney? Who?

HARTWELL: Powell said it was a start. But he wants to maintain deniability.

AMIRA: *(Contemptuously)* Deniability.

HARTWELL: Shimon Peres liked it. He gave it his blessing.

AMIRA: Then who said no?

HARTWELL: Guess.

AMIRA: Sharon.

HARTWELL: Dismissed it out of hand.

AMIRA: Who presented it to him?

HARTWELL: One of his subordinates.

AMIRA: Not you?

HARTWELL: They wouldn't let me. I asked if I could at least be in the room to answer his arguments. They refused.

AMIRA: Why?

HARTWELL: I don't know.

AMIRA: I do. It's the company you keep.

HARTWELL: That might be part of it.

AMIRA: That might be a large part of it. Well I'm sorry. All my life I have refused to hide under the chador. If I'm to blame, so be it.

HARTWELL: You've done what you could, Amira.

AMIRA: Did Sharon know it was endorsed by Arafat?

HARTWELL: That was another strike against it.

AMIRA: Of course, of course. So did you hear any other objections?

HARTWELL: It was the issue of security.

AMIRA: Security? Good Lord, does he realize that this is the first time since the establishment of the state of Israel that we are willing to renounce the right of return.

HARTWELL: Sharon doesn't trust us, Amira. Or if he does, he doesn't want to pay the price.

AMIRA: The price? The price is simply the settlements. We take them over. We occupy their houses just as they've occupied ours. We both accept the 1967 boundary endorsed by the United Nations. We share Jerusalem. We divide the water rights— fairly. It's simple, it's just, it's permanent.

HARTWELL: They're worried about terrorists.

AMIRA: And we're worried about the settlers. Surely they're equivalent. So we both crack down.

HARTWELL: It was a lovely plan. But obviously naive. *(He tosses the Peace Plan aside. During the rest of the scene he takes off his jacket, removes his tie, loosens his shirt.)*

AMIRA: Why do they have to have a Jewish state anyway? When your forefathers established the United States, they prevented it from becoming a strictly Christian country.

HARTWELL: I'm beginning to wonder if they succeeded.

AMIRA: But they saw the dangers of religion. It's in your constitution.

HARTWELL: Israel is different.

AMIRA: Oh yes. They have no constitution at all.

HARTWELL: No, I meant....

AMIRA: I know, I know. The Holocaust. Oh, Hartwell, how could your American Jews let this happen? They have thrived in your country. They have become the most generous, articulate, peace-loving and morally aware people in the entire world. How can they stand by while Israel behaves this way? Please explain this to me.

HARTWELL: O K. Here's what I think. You're right: American Jews have thrived. They have risen to the top in almost every field of endeavor they've put their hand to. But over all their successes hovers the Holocaust, like a great, dank cloud. Support for Israel allows them to reconcile everything they've accomplished in America with their deep need to expiate everything that happened in Europe.

AMIRA: And the Palestinian people, who had nothing to do with any of this, end up bearing the brunt.

HARTWELL: I don't know. The more I think about it, the more I know I don't know.... Hey, any chance of getting a drink here in this doomed domicile? Or is alcohol totally taboo?

AMIRA: *(Indicating prop table)* Help yourself.

(He goes to fix himself a drink.)

AMIRA: At least some good will come from all your labors. You can comfort yourself with that.

HARTWELL: What good?

AMIRA: You've prevented an act of terrorism in America.

HARTWELL: Have I?

AMIRA: Surely you've made use of what my son told you.

HARTWELL: All he told me, Amira, was that there's to be some kind of attack. Probably by air. Probably in September. Probably on some major city along the East Coast.

AMIRA: And you passed it on?

HARTWELL: Of course. And followed it up the line.

AMIRA: And what did they say?

HARTWELL: They said thank you.

AMIRA: That's all?

HARTWELL: They get these warnings all the time, Amira.

AMIRA: Maybe, but not from such a source.

HARTWELL: They questioned the source.

AMIRA: Did you say he has a special feeling for America?

HARTWELL: Words to that effect...

AMIRA: Did you say you met him personally? Did you tell them what you told me, that he was an exceptional young man?

HARTWELL: I said all that, Amira.

AMIRA: And it was true, wasn't it? You did like him?

HARTWELL: All the time I was with him, I kept thinking....

(Pause)

AMIRA: You kept thinking what?

HARTWELL: This is dumb, I guess, but I kept thinking that in a different world he and I might be hitting a tennis ball on the clay courts of the American University, overlooking the harbor at Beirut.

AMIRA: You see? You thought of him as your son. You should have told them that. Maybe they would have trusted him more.

HARTWELL: Maybe they would have thrown me out of the room.

AMIRA: This is agony! Whatever horror they're
planning for your country might be avoided if
we had peace in mine.

HARTWELL: I wonder.

AMIRA: What do I tell my son, then?

HARTWELL: *(Pouring another drink)* Tell him I've turned
to drink.

AMIRA: Hartwell.

HARTWELL: Tell him we tried our damnedest.

AMIRA: He was terribly invested in this. What will he
do now? Where will he go?

HARTWELL: I hope not back to Hamas.

AMIRA: Who knows? Oh this breaks my heart.

HARTWELL: Amira. *(He puts his arm around her.)*

AMIRA: And what about us? What do we do next?
I suppose I'll have to return to Ramallah, and march
in protests, and ride in ambulances with our wounded
children, and send frantic faxes to human rights
organizations, and pray to God almost as if I believed
in him. And you? You climb into your silver plane,
and retreat to Washington, and settle in behind your
big desk.

HARTWELL: I won't be settling behind my desk.
They've asked for my resignation.

AMIRA: No!

HARTWELL: I've been characterized as a loose cannon.
Which means...

AMIRA: I know what it means.

HARTWELL: I am guilty of—let's see. How did it go?—
"using my position to lend legitimacy to a half-baked
proposal which reflects neither a knowledge of the

region nor the approval of my superiors." Something like that.

AMIRA: Our lovely peace plan.

HARTWELL: I was also reprimanded for inappropriate personal contacts.... So, in a couple of weeks, a State Department spokesman will make a brief announcement that I've submitted my resignation, in order to spend more time with my family. This, as my wife sues for divorce, and my two children loll around Los Angeles, "developing" screenplays which I imagine are saturated with the violence and vulgarity of contemporary American life....

AMIRA: I suppose it was the Jews who had you fired.

HARTWELL: Not at all. My Republican buddies did me in.

AMIRA: Because they needed Jewish financial support.

HARTWELL: No, they were right to fire me. I'm not the guy they appointed, Amira. I'm different now. I *am* a loose cannon. I sense it, they sense it, even my wife sensed it. She thinks it has to do with you. Which is ironic, because this hasn't been about sex at all.

AMIRA: Did you tell her that?

HARTWELL: She wouldn't have believed me.

AMIRA: What will this different man do now?

HARTWELL: Tomorrow? I don't know. Tonight I want to go to bed with you.

AMIRA: How could we possibly make love, when all our work has come to nothing?

HARTWELL: In college, we read some French philosopher who wrote that despair is the greatest aphrodisiac. Do you agree with that?

AMIRA: Perhaps that's why we Palestinians have so many children.

HARTWELL: So what say we spend the night together. At least for old times' sake. I don't think I love you, and I'm pretty sure you don't love me, but I'll bet we could still have a pretty good time in the sack.

AMIRA: Will your staff report this to Washington?

HARTWELL: Immediately. But hell, I might as well be hung for a sheep as for a lamb.

AMIRA: Now that expression I've never understood. Sheep? Lamb?

HARTWELL: Not important. Just think of me as an old goat.

(They embrace.)

(Blackout, then SALLY *comes on)*

(Time: September 11, 2001)

SALLY: *(Entering; to audience)* Someone once tried to write a movie based on this play. The screenplay takes us all over the world, and becomes too much of a travelogue, but it does contain one sequence which might work better than the stage version. Here's how it goes: London, late afternoon, early September. ...Sally is at the sweater counter at Harrod's, doing some shopping for the holidays before heading home. I become aware of a peculiar buzz in the store, and people scurrying down the aisles, so I join the stampede. The camera follows me up the escalator to the third floor where the television sets are sold. And there it is, in all its horror, on banks of monitors, large and small, over and over, all around us...the planes hitting, the firemen and the police, the people running, the buildings collapsing, the clouds of dust, the whole ghastly nightmare. ...Cut to me stumbling out onto the street. I take out my cell phone, try to call my parents in New York. ...I can't get through.

(SWING ACTORS *come on as young American tourists,* CHRIS *and* ANNIE.)

SALLY: This young couple comes up to me.

CHRIS: Excuse me, Miss. You're American, aren't you?

SALLY: I sure am.

ANNIE: Have you heard?

SALLY: It's horrible.

ANNIE: We were flying home from Amsterdam, but our plane was diverted to Heathrow.

CHRIS: Nothing is landing along the entire East Coast.

SALLY: I can't get through on my cell.

ANNIE: *(Breaking down)* We just had this urge to be with another American.

SALLY: *(arm around her)* My hotel is right around the corner. Let's hunker down at the bar.

SALLY: Cut to us settling at a table and ordering pints. The camera pans around the room. We see various other Americans, fussing with their cell phones or checking their airline tickets, obviously stranded like ourselves.

ANNIE: Above the bar, C N N repeats and repeats silent images of the disaster.

SALLY: We sip our beer, and stare at the T V, and then try not to stare at it.

ANNIE: And soon the other Americans come over....

CHRIS: Pull up a chair, we say ...

ANNIE: There's plenty of room.

SALLY: So they do. We all kind of huddle together.

CHRIS: One of them is a woman who digs around in her purse and comes up with a little American flag which she got in some souvenir shop.

SALLY: She proudly waves it around.

CHRIS: Close-up of hand waving flag. Pull back to show us all giving her thumbs-up....

SALLY: And feeling proudly American...

CHRIS: And the camera pans around again.

SALLY: And now we see other people, watching us, and nodding sympathetically, and giving us the V sign....

ANNIE: An older English couple comes over to express their sympathies and regrets.

CHRIS: "Join us," we say.

ANNIE: So they sit down.

SALLY: And some Japanese tourists come over.

CHRIS: And some Polish students...

ANNIE: And everyone pulls up chairs.

SALLY: And the British couple mention the London Blitz. And the Japanese bring up Hiroshima. And the Poles talk about being invaded and reinvaded for three hundred years....

CHRIS: And then even the bartender comes over....

ANNIE: He's Pakistani....

SALLY: And he describes the partition of India, where thousands of people were killed in one night....

ANNIE: And then I say that I don't feel quite so American any more.

CHRIS: I add that American isn't quite the right word.

SALLY: So I tell the lady to please stop waving that flag. "Put that thing away," I say. "We are all in this thing together" ... Which I hope you'll notice is a line which Hartwell has used twice before.

CHRIS: So now we're seeing all these people from all these different countries....

ANNIE: Countries that have been hit, at one time or another...

CHRIS: Various citizens , living in a dangerous world, which you know will become more dangerous in the future...

ANNIE: And you can tell that we all feel a kind of love for each other....

CHRIS: Well, not love...

ANNIE: Yes, love. Whenever I play this scene, I feel love....

CHRIS: Oh Christ, not love. Sympathy maybe. Fellowship perhaps.

ANNIE: No, it's more than that. It's love!

CHRIS: You see what you do? Every time you make it too goddam sentimental!

ANNIE: That happens to be how I feel!

SALLY: *(Intervening)* The point is, the screenplay made it a very moving scene.... *(To audience)* Much more moving than some dumb stage version where the actors just stand around and tell you about it.

(Sound: a telephone ringing)

SALLY: But there's my phone, back in my office in Washington, several weeks later....

(She goes to answer. SWING ACTOR, *now as her* ASSISTANT, *hands her a phone.)*

(Time: Late September, 2001)

SALLY: Yes?...

ASSISTANT: Some woman with a foreign accent.
Named Elmira or something.

SALLY: Amira?

ASSISTANT: That's sounds right.,

SALLY: Oh boy... Put her on.

(ASSISTANT *goes off as* AMIRA *comes on with cell phone.*)

AMIRA: May I call you Sally?

SALLY: Everyone does.

AMIRA: I am Amira.

SALLY: I've heard about you....

AMIRA: He's told you?

SALLY: Many times.

AMIRA: He has also spoken to me about you.

SALLY: I doubt quite as much.

AMIRA: Ah well.

SALLY: Say, are you calling all the way from Palestine?

AMIRA: I am in New York. I am a guest of the
Palestinian Observer Mission at the United Nations.
I have come to see Hartwell Clark.

SALLY: Good luck.

AMIRA: But I can't locate him. His telephone is
disconnected.

SALLY: I know.

AMIRA: You've been trying, too?

SALLY: Oh sure...

AMIRA: The State Department won't tell me anything.

SALLY: Because they don't know anything.

AMIRA: I even called his wife.

SALLY: And she hung up on you.

AMIRA: You, too?

SALLY: Oh yes.

AMIRA: But he should be speaking out. The people of Palestine gave his government a specific warning of the September attacks.

SALLY: That I didn't know.

AMIRA: Hartwell knows. He should be shouting it to the world!

SALLY: Hartwell doesn't shout.

AMIRA: Then he should whisper it to the newspapers. Or has he been bought off by the Jews?

SALLY: Oh please.

AMIRA: Or by the Bush family.

SALLY: There's a thought.

AMIRA: He should go on television, and demand that Israel enter new peace talks immediately. Otherwise there will be more attacks. I am absolutely convinced of it!

SALLY: I wish I could help.

AMIRA: I was hoping you could.

SALLY: We decided to finish this scene without having to hold these stupid gadgets to our ears.

(*They hand off their phones.*)

SALLY: Look...

AMIRA: May I say something personal?

SALLY: Go ahead.

AMIRA: I was very jealous of you, once upon a time.

SALLY: Jealous?

AMIRA: I thought you were the one he came home to.

SALLY: Not a chance.

AMIRA: Were you ever jealous of me?

SALLY: Still am.

AMIRA: There's no need.

SALLY: I'm not so sure.

AMIRA: I have no room in my heart for love.

SALLY: Oh now...

AMIRA: My heart has turned to stone.

SALLY: Don't say that.

AMIRA: But you. He used to talk about you all the time. "My friend Sally thinks this. My friend Sally thinks that." He said you were always his guiding star.

SALLY: Guiding star?

AMIRA: I thought you might guide me to him.

SALLY: Gee.

AMIRA: Well. Now I must say goodbye. *(Starts out)*

SALLY: Amira...

(AMIRA *stops.)*

SALLY: Did Hartwell ever mention New Hampshire?

AMIRA: New Hampshire?

SALLY: His grandfather's farm?

AMIRA: No.

SALLY: An old house on a lake? No telephone, no electricity? Trout fishing? He never talked about that?

AMIRA: Not with me.

SALLY: He took me up there once. To fish, I hasten to add.

AMIRA: You think that's where he is?

SALLY: I think he loved it there.

AMIRA: Then I shall go there.

SALLY: It could be just a wild goose chase.

AMIRA: Wild goose—?

SALLY: Never mind. Now if I remember correctly, you take the Middlesex Turnpike north from Boston and turn off by this diner onto a road with an Indian name...Pentacook, I think it was....

AMIRA: *(To audience)* ...And she told me to go to the town with the same name, which had a general store where you could get further directions....

(Time: Late September)

(Card: autumn colors; a lovely lake; mountains behind)

(SALLY and AMIRA go off as HARTWELL comes on, upstage, with fly rod and fishing gear.)

HARTWELL: My grandfather was born up here. After he made his pile, he bought it back, and all the land around it, including the lake....

(Sound: bird calls, the call of a loon, an occasional splash)

HARTWELL: ...which had the finest trout-fishing east of the Adirondacks. Nowadays, the caretaker puts a ton of lime on the ice every winter. Which melts into the lake every spring. And counteracts the effects of acid rain... The fishing is good, but not what it used to be.

(He goes as AMIRA comes on. She still wears her high heels, carries her purse.)

AMIRA: *(To herself)* Look at this lake! *(Over her shoulder)* Please come here and look at this lake.

(SWING ACTOR, *in a dark driver's cap, comes on as*
NATHAN, *an Israeli driver from a New York car service.*)

NATHAN: Are we here?

AMIRA: I believe so. *(She looks at her written directions.)*
They said at the store to turn right at the old barn....

NATHAN: Which we did...

AMIRA: Two and a half miles up the dirt road...

NATHAN: I'm charging you depreciation for that road.

AMIRA: You're not serious.

NATHAN: You may argue it out with Tel Aviv Car
Service when we return to New York.

AMIRA: I certainly intend to. Meanwhile look at the
lake...

(They look.)

NATHAN: What do we now?

AMIRA: We call. *(Calling out)* Hartwell Clark!...
Clark...Clark!

(An echo effect to give a sense of space and distance)

AMIRA: Hello! *(To* NATHAN*)* Help me, please.
You've got a loud voice.

NATHAN: Thank you for the compliment. *(Calling)*
Hello!... 'lo...lo...

AMIRA: I heard something.

NATHAN: I didn't.

AMIRA: That's because you're quite deaf. I noticed it
driving up. You didn't hear half the things I said to you.

NATHAN: Perhaps I didn't want to hear them.

AMIRA: That's the trouble with you Jews. You hear only
what you want to hear. *(Calling)* Hartwell! ...'well...'well!

NATHAN: Why didn't you phone ahead?

AMIRA: I keep telling you. There's no telephone here.

NATHAN: Maybe he's not here.

AMIRA: He has to be. It's inevitable.

NATHAN: That's the trouble with you Arabs. You think everything is inevitable.

AMIRA: It's inevitable we have a homeland.

NATHAN: That depends what you mean by homeland.

AMIRA: I refuse to argue.

NATHAN: This is something new.

AMIRA: Never mind. Look at this lake! I've never seen so much water in my life.

NATHAN: You flew over the entire Atlantic Ocean.

AMIRA: I am speaking of fresh water, my dear sir. I am speaking of water for drinking. And supporting a civilization. Like the Sea of Galilee. Which the Palestinian people no longer have access to.

NATHAN: You get water rights.

AMIRA: Hardly enough. I have seen Jewish women in the settlements sunning themselves by their swimming pools, while behind a chain-link fence, Palestinian women line up to catch a few drops of rusty water from a broken pipe.

NATHAN: Maybe Arafat should fix that pipe, instead of buying weapons from Iran.

AMIRA: Maybe Israel, which gets ten million dollars a day from the United States government, should stop spending it on swimming pools for their illegal settlements.

(HARTWELL *comes on, with his fishing gear.*)

HARTWELL: Good Lord! Look who's here!

AMIRA: I have tracked you down!

HARTWELL: *(Kissing her)* You sure did. The big question is how?

NATHAN: *(Indian sign)* How...

AMIRA: This is the Tel Aviv Car Service.

NATHAN: I am a citizen of Israel. I have a son studying at Pomona College in California.

AMIRA: We have argued politics all the way up.

NATHAN: We have agreed to disagree.

AMIRA: We have agreed to nothing.

NATHAN: You see how the Arabs respond to our peaceful overtures?

HARTWELL: How the hell did you find me, Amira?

AMIRA: Through your friend Sally.

HARTWELL: Ah. Right. Sally would know. ...Well, now you're here, look what I've got. *(Displays his fishing basket)* Trout. Last of the season. One for each of us. Stay for dinner.

AMIRA: I am here only to talk, Hartwell.

HARTWELL: Just talk?

NATHAN: She talks continually.

HARTWELL: O K. But we have a rule up here. If people want to talk, they have to sit and watch the sunset while they're doing it. *(He brings a couple of lawn chairs down; to* NATHAN*)* Get yourself a chair.

AMIRA: I don't want him here. Like most Jews, he tries to dominate the conversation.

NATHAN: Like most Israelis, I yearn for a moment of peaceful solitude ... I'll go nap in the car. *(Goes off)*

AMIRA: That man is impossible. Shouts, argues, won't listen to reason.

HARTWELL: As opposed to your quiet, measured, subtle style of discourse? Have a seat. *(He leads her to a chair.)*

AMIRA: *(Not sitting)* I'm very disappointed in you, Hartwell.

HARTWELL: How about a drink?

AMIRA: I don't drink, as you very well know....

HARTWELL: Now you're in the U S, I should think you'd be tempted to take it up. *(Pouring himself a drink)* A good Scotch after a good catch is a sportsman's necessity. And since another rule around here is that you can't drink alone, I'll give you a vintage bottle of Hires' Root Beer which has been aging in the New Hampshire woods for at least ten years.

AMIRA: Hartwell, please. I'm in no mood for these rhetorical flourishes.

HARTWELL: Can't you see I'm stalling? ...

(They sit.)

HARTWELL: My grandfather built several fancy houses during his life, but liked it best right here, where he was born. He caught fish from the lake, grew vegetables in the garden, and tried to live off the land. The modern world cuts you off from the heartbeat of life, he'd tell us. Up here you renew your roots.

AMIRA: Which is why the Jews go to Israel, I suppose.

HARTWELL: Exactly. Good for you, Amira...

AMIRA: And why the Palestinians yearn for their homeland....

HARTWELL: O K, O K.

AMIRA: But no more ancient history, please. I want to know why you're here.

HARTWELL: I needed to lick my wounds after nine-eleven.

AMIRA: You were hardly the one who was wounded.

HARTWELL: I was the one who messed up. When I got fired, I thought O K, sorry, I tried, but whatever they want, they obviously don't want me. I was the good, well-bred WASP who bowed out with a polite cover story. But when the planes hit, and the towers collapsed, and all those people were killed, I knew I might have prevented it.

AMIRA: How could you possibly?

HARTWELL: By pounding the table and raising the roof!

AMIRA: You can do that now.

HARTWELL: Too late, too late, too goddam late!

AMIRA: Not at all. Come down with me, right now. We'll call a press conference. You can announce to the world that the Palestinian people gave you ample warning. You can insist that Israel resume peace talks immediately, with the clear promise of a Palestinian state.

HARTWELL: Yeah, right. A half-assed plea, week after the fact, by a fired functionary, leading—if I'm lucky—to a small sound-bite on C N N after a Viagra commercial. Oh Amira, the world has spun past all that. We're now deep into the next period. After some open-field running in Afghanistan, we're planning to crash through the line on Iraq.

AMIRA: All the more reason not to retreat to the woods, Hartwell Clark.

HARTWELL: Retreat, hell. Look what I've been doing. *(He gets a backpack.)* Reading. Studying. Learning. *(Takes out book after book)* You can't talk about the Jews without reading their history. And you can't talk about the Middle East without studying Islam. And then you look at secondary sources on both. After that, you might be able to write something down. *(Takes out a pad of paper with some writing on it)*

AMIRA: *(Taking it)* And what, pray tell, is this?

HARTWELL: A book. I'm writing a book.

AMIRA: A rather small book, I might say....

HARTWELL: Oh that's just notes and questions. When I'm farther along, I'll hire a graduate student to keep me honest, and a ghost writer to keep me clear.

AMIRA: Am I in this book?

HARTWELL: No way. Sorry. Nothing personal allowed. This will be a carefully reasoned argument from beginning to end, leading to a fair and just peace plan for the entire Middle East. And when I've got it right, I'll get it published.

AMIRA: Oh you will, will you?

HARTWELL: Sure. A classmate of mine from Yale is a major editor at Random House. He likes the idea.

AMIRA: So when may we hope to expect this solution to all our problems?

HARTWELL: In a couple of years, more or less. Probably more, if I'm going to get it right.

(It's darker now.)

AMIRA: Meanwhile my people die every day. What do I do in the meantime, Hartwell? What do I do?

HARTWELL: You do what you're good at, Amira. You continue to scream bloody murder. And for a moment, you can relax and watch the sun go down.

(They sit and watch, for a moment. Cricket sounds, loons)

AMIRA: Oh you nature-loving Americans, with your Thoreaus and your Hemingways.

HARTWELL: Ssssh. Listen...

(Distant sound of splashing)

HARTWELL: Hear that? That's a raccoon who brings her family down every night to fish for frogs. Life goes on, Amira. Life goes on.

(They look. Then suddenly there is the strident sound of a cell phone ringing.)

HARTWELL: Good Lord. What's that?

AMIRA: *(Getting her phone from her purse)* My cellular phone. *(She answers.)* Yes?... *(She begins to speak rapid Arabic.)* Hada ana. *("This is she." Pause)* la...Waktaish... sha-yiff? *("Oh no... When?...You see what happens?" Pause)* Ana khalbi mahrouk. *("Oh my heart is broken.")* *(She slowly puts the phone back in her purse.)* I would like to have a drink now, thank you, Hartwell.

HARTWELL: An alcoholic beverage?

AMIRA: Please.

HARTWELL: *(Handing her his own drink)* Trouble?

AMIRA: Yes. *(Taking a sip)* While we've been sitting here, discussing the beauties of nature and the pleasures of careful scholarship... *(Another sip)* My son, my only son, my dear, dear son, has just blown himself up, along with two Israeli soldiers, at a checkpoint on the road to Jerusalem.

HARTWELL: No.

AMIRA: So much for your reasoned argument, Hartwell.

HARTWELL: *(Looking at "book")* This is horse shit, isn't it?

AMIRA: It is to me.

(NATHAN *comes back on.*)

NATHAN: Did I hear a phone somewhere?

HARTWELL: We've had bad news.

AMIRA: My son is dead.

NATHAN: The boy you told me about?

HARTWELL: Suicide bomb.

NATHAN: How many Jews?

HARTWELL: Two. *(Pause)* Soldiers. *(Pause)* I knew him, you know.

NATHAN: You knew her son?

HARTWELL: He was my son, too! *(He goes off hurriedly.)*

AMIRA: I want to go back.

NATHAN: Take my arm. It's rough walking here.

AMIRA: *(Taking his arm)* Thank you, sir.

NATHAN: Let me say this: I'm very sorry. This is a terrible thing.

AMIRA: Would you like to know something even more terrible? I don't know whether I'm sorry or not.

(They go off together. A moment. Then HARTWELL *comes out of the house. Crumbling his notes, he gives a great cry of despair.)*

(Blackout)

(Time: December, 2001)

(Sound: a Christmas carol: God Rest Ye, Merry Gentlemen, Let Nothing You Dismay*)*

*(*SALLY *comes on.)*

SALLY: And now, heeere's Sally, once again picking up the pieces. *(She picks up the books and the scattered pages from the New Hampshire scene.)*

*(Card: a large Christmas tree ornament decorated with the
Star of David)*

SALLY: *(To audience)* We are now in New York, where
I've been visiting my parents over the holidays—
and moderating the annual argument over whether to
have a tree. And look what showed up in the Christmas
mail... *(She is handed a FedEx envelope, which she opens.)*
A book! Or sort of a book. More like a pamphlet, really.
(Displaying a large, messy clipped-together stack of papers)
Written by Hartwell Clark, Former United States
Deputy Assistant etcetera etcetera.

(Card: a page from the manuscript is displayed)

SALLY: See? Look. Riddled with typos. And corrections
all over the margins. Obviously written in haste.
And the letter "H" is virtually non-existent throughout.
I'll bet he typed it with one finger on some rusty old
typewriter, up in New Hampshire. *(Displays a scrawled
note)* And there's a note attached. Saying he's coming
down to New York and needs my opinion immediately.
So I've been up all night reading the damn thing.
And before I could get my second cup of coffee.

(HARTWELL hurries on, still in jeans and flannel shirt.)

HARTWELL: *(Handing her a coffee)* What do you think?

SALLY: It's a Jeremiad, Hartwell.

HARTWELL: Say again?

SALLY: A Jeremiad. A lamentation. A song of woe.
Like the prophet Jeremiah.

HARTWELL: You mean, I'm now sounding Jewish?

SALLY: You're sounding more like your Puritan
forefathers. I see you as one of those old New England
ministers staggering to the pulpit after an Indian attack,
and announcing to the congregation that they were
being punished because of their sins.

HARTWELL: Oh come on.

SALLY: You go after our entire way of life. You indict us up and down the line! As for terrorism, you say we're asking for it.

HARTWELL: Well we are.

SALLY: Pick a page, any page. *(Flips through the pages, reads at random)* "We boast about the glories of capitalism and democracy, but by our works shall ye know us. Consider the disgusting gap between our rich and our poor."

HARTWELL: It's true, isn't it?

SALLY: *(Reading on)* "Or look at our culture. Our films celebrate the destruction of everything we've been told to value, while our television urges us to buy stuff we know we don't need..." You go on and on.

HARTWELL: I've been on a roll. I wrote the whole thing in eight weeks.

SALLY: It shows.

HARTWELL: Do you think it will cause a major furor when it's published?

SALLY: Nope.

HARTWELL: No?

SALLY: No publisher will touch it, Hartwell.

HARTWELL: You mean because I nail the Israelis?

SALLY: You're just as tough on the Palestinians.

HARTWELL: Glad you noticed.

SALLY: The real problem comes when you start nailing yourself.

HARTWELL: Why is that a problem? I've been an asshole most of my life.

SALLY: You go on to say we're all assholes.

HARTWELL: We are! We run around living these loud, arrogant, extravagant lives, while half of the world lives no life at all. We provoke envy, frustration, and anger wherever we go.

SALLY: The poor are always with us, Hartwell.

HARTWELL: But today they're with us so much more! Or rather we're with *them*. In their face. We assault them day and night with movies and television to remind them of a phony life that they can't even hope to have! All we do is humiliate them.

SALLY: So? You want us to make better movies and fewer commercials?

HARTWELL: I want us to change our ways. Unless we do, there are sure to be more attacks on American lives and property at home and abroad. We are in the last stages of capitalism, Sally. Our executives are corrupt, our workers frustrated, our products unnecessary, and our consumers...do you like being called a consumer, Sally? Do you like being defined by how much you *consume*? Do you like being told by the President of the United States after the September attacks that the best thing you can do is go out and buy stuff?

SALLY: No I do not.

HARTWELL: Oh God, we are a sick society. Bush says we're at war against terrorism, but I say that this is no war. We are fighting a disease, Sally. Terrorism is the cancer of a corrupt capitalism. Meanwhile we go on living showy, frivolous, dissolute lives. We've been diagnosed with lung cancer, but still go around sucking on cigarettes.

SALLY: And what do you propose we do about it, Mr Secretary?

HARTWELL: Well, you'll be glad to hear that I've started by trading in my S U V for a Honda hybrid.

SALLY: Oh terrific. *(Indicating manuscript)* You are challenging the whole American Dream....

HARTWELL: Whatever that is.

SALLY: *(Finding a passage, reading)* "What's so hot about America anyway?"

HARTWELL: Let me do it. I know it cold. *(Recites from memory)* "What's so hot about America, anyway? What's so great about the lives we lead? Our seniors are depressed, our children flabby and morose, our very dreams corrupted with money. When you boil it down, there are only two ultimately important things about the United States of America: one, the variety, beauty, and bounty of our land, and two, our Constitution with its Bill of Rights. And Bush is fast undermining both."

SALLY: This is tough stuff, Hartwell.

HARTWELL: I FedExed a copy to Amira.

SALLY: Don't be hurt if you don't hear from her.

HARTWELL: Why wouldn't I?

SALLY: Because she'll think you're nuts.

HARTWELL: Do you?

SALLY: I refuse to answer on the grounds that—

HARTWELL: No, no. The reason I won't hear from Amira is that she's a nationalist at heart. She wants a Palestinian state. And I'm beginning to think that nationalism is a thing of the past.

SALLY: Tell the Israelis that.

HARTWELL: I will! I'll put that in. I'll say...I'll say that Israel is a nineteenth-century solution to a twentieth-century crime. How about that?

SALLY: Beautifully put.

HARTWELL: Yes well we're in a new century, now, Sally. The nation-state is just a stepping stone to a larger vision of the human community. We are all in this thing together. Who is my brother? Every man is my brother. Amira's son was my son.

SALLY: *(To audience)* Here's where he tells me about that poor boy who blew himself up.

HARTWELL: That was my son.

SALLY: It's a sweet thought, at least.

HARTWELL: You really think I'm nuts?

SALLY: I really think you're somewhat wound up.

HARTWELL: Last week the caretaker up at the cottage stopped by to help me split firewood, and after five minutes of conversation, he said I should "see someone" quote unquote. This hick New Hampshire farmer thinks I need a shrink.

SALLY: I tend to agree.

HARTWELL: O K, so my book won't be published. So what? I'll learn to do the desktop thing, whatever that means. Print it up, send it out myself...

SALLY: Hartwell, sweetie, I'm not sure anyone will want to read it.

HARTWELL: Oh a few will, won't they? I'll send it around to people I know. Maybe they'll glance at it, talk about it, pass it on. And I'll make speeches about it. Stand on soap boxes in public squares...

SALLY: Soap comes as liquid detergent these days, Hartwell. And where are the public squares?

HARTWELL: You're so goddam negative, Sal!

SALLY: Oh am I really?

HARTWELL: Yes!

SALLY: Well good for me! It's about time! For how
many years have I listened to you sound off? From
college on, for Christ sake! It seems for centuries I
have sat there, with my knees together, saying "That's
interesting" or "Yes, but" or "Have you considered"
while you tell me what you're studying and who you're
going to marry and how you plan to save the Middle
East. But now I have to be *enthusiastic*? Now I have to
jump up and down? Over this weird diatribe that
you've been downloading on me even before breakfast?
No thank you, Hartwell. I happen to agree with some of
what you say, but half the time I think you're full of shit!

HARTWELL: You've just given me a title.

SALLY: I don't care.

HARTWELL: I'm calling it "O Jerusalem."

SALLY: It's already been used.

HARTWELL: Not the way I'll use it. Because you've
just shown me that Jerusalem is more than just a
geographical place, Sally. It also means something
personal. For example, what if you're my Jerusalem,
and I'm yours?

(Another pause)

SALLY: Let's have lunch, Hartwell.

HARTWELL: What if you're here to bring me down,
and I'm here to stir you up?

SALLY: I said let's have lunch.

HARTWELL: Today?

SALLY: Today.

HARTWELL: Can't.

SALLY: What? You can't? Do you realize this is the first time in our long relationship that I'm actually making the first move, and you're blowing me off?

HARTWELL: I signed up to give a noonday talk at the Yale Club.

SALLY: Why, for God's sake?

HARTWELL: So I can call on the Old Boy network. They're always there when the chips are down.

SALLY: You'll get killed, Hartwell.

HARTWELL: At the Yale Club?

SALLY: Figuratively speaking,

HARTWELL: Then come along and protect me.

SALLY: I couldn't stand it.

HARTWELL: So long then. *(Giving her a quick kiss)* I'll be back later.

SALLY: Oh sure. Any day. Story of my life.

(HARTWELL *goes;* SALLY *looks after him.)*

(Time: the future)

(SWING ACTRESS *comes on)*

SWING ACTRESS: *(To audience)* The original ending to this play is composed of a series of quick scenes, concluding with the death of Hartwell Clark.

SALLY: Hey wait! Not so fast there, lady. *(To audience)* First he gets kicked out of the Yale Club, so we *do* go out for lunch, and after that, guess what? Audience, I married him!

(She is brought a bucket and some gardening gloves.)

SALLY: We go to live on that farm in New Hampshire. We fish, grow organic vegetables, and raise Labrador Retrievers. And I have to tell you there's nothing closer

to heaven than rolling around in a fresh-cut New
Hampshire field with a litter of Labs and the man you
love...

SWING ACTRESS: Maybe the play should end here...

SALLY: But it doesn't. Here's what happens next.

(HARTWELL *comes back on.*)

HARTWELL: (*Handing off the rake*) It's not enough, is it?

SALLY: Cultivating our own garden?

HARTWELL: I've got to make more speeches.

SALLY: Oh no!

HARTWELL: Got to do it, Sal. Got to change the world.
(*Kisses her*) Goodbye, love, once again. (*He goes to stand
behind her, holding her.*)

SWING ACTRESS: So he gives speeches all over the
country. And sooner or later, he ends up giving a
lecture back in Houston, where during the Q and A,
he is shot through the heart by some crazy right-winger
who has brought a perfectly legal concealed weapon to
the lecture hall.

(HARTWELL *exits.*)

SALLY: So the original play ends with me, Sally, giving
a sweet, sad speech at his graveside, a la *Death of a
Salesman*. I'd do it for you now, but I always cry.
(*She hurries off.*)

SWING ACTRESS: (*To audience; quickly*) This happens
occasionally, so we've worked up two short codas
of our own. This one takes place sometime in the
future... (*She becomes a University official.*) This year,
the University of Jerusalem awards the medal of
distinction to the Minister of Education for the
Federated Republic of Israel-Palestine.

(*Sound: applause.* SWING ACTRESS *gives the medallion to* AMIRA, *now in cap and gown.*)

AMIRA: I accept this medal proudly on behalf of our combined constituencies. But I must say this: we will never be a successful confederation until our schools dispense with religion in the classroom. I will fight for that end as long as I live.

(*Sound: applause*)

SWING ACTOR: (*To audience*) And here's another, which is set even farther along in time. (*He is handed a neat, important-looking document. Reads to audience*) As Secretary-General of the United Citizens of the World, I should like to conclude our celebration of permanent peace by asking Mrs Sally Clark to lead us in a responsive reading of the opening sentence of the preamble to our common constitution, which is taken directly from her husband's seminal work, "O Jerusalem." (*Toward off*) You're on, Sally.

(SALLY *comes back on, blowing her nose, takes the document.*)

SALLY: (*Reading*) "In order to form a more perfect world..."

OTHER ACTORS: "...That we may enjoy the fruits of peace and plenteousness..."

SALLY: "We hold this truth to be self-evident...."

(HARTWELL *rejoins the group, stands at the center.*)

ALL: "...That we are all in this thing together!"

SALLY: (*To audience*) So that's how we end this play— at least for now.

(*Music*) (*The actors go off together.*)

(*Curtain*)

END OF PLAY

www.ingramcontent.com/pod-product-compliance
Lightning Source LLC
Chambersburg PA
CBHW061044050726
47592CB00004B/1592